SWIM LOGBOOK

NAME:

E-MAIL: PHONE:

ADDRESS:

SWIM LOG

DATE: .... TIME: ....

BEGINNER ◯ INTERMEDIATE ◯ ADVANCED ◯

WARM UP	REPS	DISTANCE	TIME

SWIMMING STYLE	REPS	DISTANCE	TIME

COOL DOWN	REPS	DISTANCE	TIME
TOTAL:			

NOTES: (TECHNIQUES, AREA OF IMPROVEMENTS, ETC.)

....

....

SWIM LOG

DATE: _____   TIME: _____

BEGINNER ◯   INTERMEDIATE ◯   ADVANCED ◯

WARM UP	REPS	DISTANCE	TIME

SWIMMING STYLE	REPS	DISTANCE	TIME

COOL DOWN	REPS	DISTANCE	TIME
TOTAL:			

NOTES: (TECHNIQUES, AREA OF IMPROVEMENTS, ETC.)

_____

_____

_____

SWIM LOG

DATE: _____ TIME: _____

BEGINNER ◯ INTERMEDIATE ◯ ADVANCED ◯

WARM UP	REPS	DISTANCE	TIME

SWIMMING STYLE	REPS	DISTANCE	TIME

COOL DOWN	REPS	DISTANCE	TIME

TOTAL:

NOTES: (TECHNIQUES, AREA OF IMPROVEMENTS, ETC.)

_____

_____

_____

SWIM LOG

DATE: _____   TIME: _____

BEGINNER ◯   INTERMEDIATE ◯   ADVANCED ◯

WARM UP	REPS	DISTANCE	TIME

SWIMMING STYLE	REPS	DISTANCE	TIME

COOL DOWN	REPS	DISTANCE	TIME

TOTAL: _____

NOTES: (TECHNIQUES, AREA OF IMPROVEMENTS, ETC.)

_____

_____

_____

SWIM LOG

DATE: _____   TIME: _____

BEGINNER ◯   INTERMEDIATE ◯   ADVANCED ◯

WARM UP	REPS	DISTANCE	TIME

SWIMMING STYLE	REPS	DISTANCE	TIME

COOL DOWN	REPS	DISTANCE	TIME
TOTAL:			

NOTES: (TECHNIQUES, AREA OF IMPROVEMENTS, ETC.)

_____

_____

_____

SWIM LOG

DATE: _____   TIME: _____

BEGINNER ◯   INTERMEDIATE ◯   ADVANCED ◯

WARM UP	REPS	DISTANCE	TIME

SWIMMING STYLE	REPS	DISTANCE	TIME

COOL DOWN	REPS	DISTANCE	TIME

TOTAL:

NOTES: (TECHNIQUES, AREA OF IMPROVEMENTS, ETC.)

_____

_____

SWIM LOG

DATE: .... TIME: ....

BEGINNER ◯   INTERMEDIATE ◯   ADVANCED ◯

WARM UP	REPS	DISTANCE	TIME

SWIMMING STYLE	REPS	DISTANCE	TIME

COOL DOWN	REPS	DISTANCE	TIME
TOTAL:			

NOTES: (TECHNIQUES, AREA OF IMPROVEMENTS, ETC.)

....

....

SWIM LOG

DATE: _____   TIME: _____

BEGINNER ⃝   INTERMEDIATE ⃝   ADVANCED ⃝

WARM UP	REPS	DISTANCE	TIME

SWIMMING STYLE	REPS	DISTANCE	TIME

COOL DOWN	REPS	DISTANCE	TIME

TOTAL:

NOTES: (TECHNIQUES, AREA OF IMPROVEMENTS, ETC.)

SWIM LOG

DATE: .... TIME: ....

BEGINNER ◯ INTERMEDIATE ◯ ADVANCED ◯

WARM UP	REPS	DISTANCE	TIME

SWIMMING STYLE	REPS	DISTANCE	TIME

COOL DOWN	REPS	DISTANCE	TIME

TOTAL:

NOTES: (TECHNIQUES, AREA OF IMPROVEMENTS, ETC.)

....

....

SWIM LOG

DATE: _____ TIME: _____

BEGINNER ⃝ INTERMEDIATE ⃝ ADVANCED ⃝

WARM UP	REPS	DISTANCE	TIME

SWIMMING STYLE	REPS	DISTANCE	TIME

COOL DOWN	REPS	DISTANCE	TIME

TOTAL:

NOTES: (TECHNIQUES, AREA OF IMPROVEMENTS, ETC.)

_____

_____

_____

SWIM LOG

DATE: _____   TIME: _____

BEGINNER ◯   INTERMEDIATE ◯   ADVANCED ◯

WARM UP	REPS	DISTANCE	TIME

SWIMMING STYLE	REPS	DISTANCE	TIME

COOL DOWN	REPS	DISTANCE	TIME

TOTAL: _____

NOTES: (TECHNIQUES, AREA OF IMPROVEMENTS, ETC.)

_____

_____

_____

SWIM LOG

DATE: _____   TIME: _____

BEGINNER ◯   INTERMEDIATE ◯   ADVANCED ◯

WARM UP	REPS	DISTANCE	TIME

SWIMMING STYLE	REPS	DISTANCE	TIME

COOL DOWN	REPS	DISTANCE	TIME

TOTAL:

NOTES: (TECHNIQUES, AREA OF IMPROVEMENTS, ETC.)

_____

_____

SWIM LOG

DATE: _____ TIME: _____

BEGINNER ⭕ INTERMEDIATE ⭕ ADVANCED ⭕

WARM UP	REPS	DISTANCE	TIME

SWIMMING STYLE	REPS	DISTANCE	TIME

COOL DOWN	REPS	DISTANCE	TIME

TOTAL:

NOTES: (TECHNIQUES, AREA OF IMPROVEMENTS, ETC.)

SWIM LOG

DATE: .... TIME: ....

BEGINNER ◯ INTERMEDIATE ◯ ADVANCED ◯

WARM UP	REPS	DISTANCE	TIME

SWIMMING STYLE	REPS	DISTANCE	TIME

COOL DOWN	REPS	DISTANCE	TIME
TOTAL:			

NOTES: (TECHNIQUES, AREA OF IMPROVEMENTS, ETC.)

....

....

....

SWIM LOG

DATE: _____ TIME: _____

BEGINNER ◯ INTERMEDIATE ◯ ADVANCED ◯

WARM UP	REPS	DISTANCE	TIME

SWIMMING STYLE	REPS	DISTANCE	TIME

COOL DOWN	REPS	DISTANCE	TIME

TOTAL: _____

NOTES: (TECHNIQUES, AREA OF IMPROVEMENTS, ETC.)

_____

_____

_____

SWIM LOG

DATE: _____   TIME: _____

BEGINNER ◯   INTERMEDIATE ◯   ADVANCED ◯

WARM UP	REPS	DISTANCE	TIME

SWIMMING STYLE	REPS	DISTANCE	TIME

COOL DOWN	REPS	DISTANCE	TIME

TOTAL:

NOTES: (TECHNIQUES, AREA OF IMPROVEMENTS, ETC.)

_____

_____

_____

SWIM LOG

DATE: _____   TIME: _____

BEGINNER ◯   INTERMEDIATE ◯   ADVANCED ◯

WARM UP	REPS	DISTANCE	TIME

SWIMMING STYLE	REPS	DISTANCE	TIME

COOL DOWN	REPS	DISTANCE	TIME

TOTAL:

NOTES: (TECHNIQUES, AREA OF IMPROVEMENTS, ETC.)

SWIM LOG

DATE: _____   TIME: _____

BEGINNER ⬤   INTERMEDIATE ⬤   ADVANCED ⬤

WARM UP	REPS	DISTANCE	TIME

SWIMMING STYLE	REPS	DISTANCE	TIME

COOL DOWN	REPS	DISTANCE	TIME
TOTAL:			

NOTES: (TECHNIQUES, AREA OF IMPROVEMENTS, ETC.)

_____

_____

_____

SWIM LOG

DATE: _____ TIME: _____

BEGINNER ◯   INTERMEDIATE ◯   ADVANCED ◯

WARM UP	REPS	DISTANCE	TIME

SWIMMING STYLE	REPS	DISTANCE	TIME

COOL DOWN	REPS	DISTANCE	TIME
TOTAL:			

NOTES: (TECHNIQUES, AREA OF IMPROVEMENTS, ETC.)

_____

_____

SWIM LOG

DATE: _____   TIME: _____

BEGINNER ⚪   INTERMEDIATE ⚪   ADVANCED ⚪

WARM UP	REPS	DISTANCE	TIME

SWIMMING STYLE	REPS	DISTANCE	TIME

COOL DOWN	REPS	DISTANCE	TIME

TOTAL: _____

NOTES: (TECHNIQUES, AREA OF IMPROVEMENTS, ETC.)

_____

_____

_____

SWIM LOG

DATE: _____   TIME: _____

BEGINNER ◯   INTERMEDIATE ◯   ADVANCED ◯

WARM UP	REPS	DISTANCE	TIME

SWIMMING STYLE	REPS	DISTANCE	TIME

COOL DOWN	REPS	DISTANCE	TIME
TOTAL:			

NOTES: (TECHNIQUES, AREA OF IMPROVEMENTS, ETC.)

_____

_____

_____

SWIM LOG

DATE: _____   TIME: _____

BEGINNER ◯   INTERMEDIATE ◯   ADVANCED ◯

WARM UP	REPS	DISTANCE	TIME

SWIMMING STYLE	REPS	DISTANCE	TIME

COOL DOWN	REPS	DISTANCE	TIME

TOTAL: _____

NOTES: (TECHNIQUES, AREA OF IMPROVEMENTS, ETC.)

_____

_____

SWIM LOG

DATE: .... TIME: ....

BEGINNER ⭕ INTERMEDIATE ⭕ ADVANCED ⭕

WARM UP	REPS	DISTANCE	TIME

SWIMMING STYLE	REPS	DISTANCE	TIME

COOL DOWN	REPS	DISTANCE	TIME
TOTAL:			

NOTES: (TECHNIQUES, AREA OF IMPROVEMENTS, ETC.)

SWIM LOG

DATE: _____   TIME: _____

BEGINNER ○   INTERMEDIATE ○   ADVANCED ○

WARM UP	REPS	DISTANCE	TIME

SWIMMING STYLE	REPS	DISTANCE	TIME

COOL DOWN	REPS	DISTANCE	TIME

TOTAL:

NOTES: (TECHNIQUES, AREA OF IMPROVEMENTS, ETC.)

_____

_____

_____

SWIM LOG

DATE: _____ TIME: _____

BEGINNER ⚪ INTERMEDIATE ⚪ ADVANCED ⚪

WARM UP	REPS	DISTANCE	TIME

SWIMMING STYLE	REPS	DISTANCE	TIME

COOL DOWN	REPS	DISTANCE	TIME
TOTAL:			

NOTES: (TECHNIQUES, AREA OF IMPROVEMENTS, ETC.)

_____

_____

_____

SWIM LOG

DATE: _____   TIME: _____

BEGINNER ◯   INTERMEDIATE ◯   ADVANCED ◯

WARM UP	REPS	DISTANCE	TIME

SWIMMING STYLE	REPS	DISTANCE	TIME

COOL DOWN	REPS	DISTANCE	TIME

TOTAL:

NOTES: (TECHNIQUES, AREA OF IMPROVEMENTS, ETC.)

_____

_____

_____

SWIM LOG

DATE: _____ TIME: _____

BEGINNER ◯   INTERMEDIATE ◯   ADVANCED ◯

WARM UP	REPS	DISTANCE	TIME

SWIMMING STYLE	REPS	DISTANCE	TIME

COOL DOWN	REPS	DISTANCE	TIME

TOTAL:

NOTES: (TECHNIQUES, AREA OF IMPROVEMENTS, ETC.)

SWIM LOG

DATE: _____   TIME: _____

BEGINNER ◯   INTERMEDIATE ◯   ADVANCED ◯

WARM UP	REPS	DISTANCE	TIME

SWIMMING STYLE	REPS	DISTANCE	TIME

COOL DOWN	REPS	DISTANCE	TIME
TOTAL:			

NOTES: (TECHNIQUES, AREA OF IMPROVEMENTS, ETC.)

_____

_____

_____

SWIM LOG

DATE: _____ TIME: _____

BEGINNER ◯ INTERMEDIATE ◯ ADVANCED ◯

WARM UP	REPS	DISTANCE	TIME

SWIMMING STYLE	REPS	DISTANCE	TIME

COOL DOWN	REPS	DISTANCE	TIME
TOTAL:			

NOTES: (TECHNIQUES, AREA OF IMPROVEMENTS, ETC.)

_____

_____

_____

SWIM LOG

DATE: _____   TIME: _____

BEGINNER ◯   INTERMEDIATE ◯   ADVANCED ◯

WARM UP	REPS	DISTANCE	TIME

SWIMMING STYLE	REPS	DISTANCE	TIME

COOL DOWN	REPS	DISTANCE	TIME

TOTAL:

NOTES: (TECHNIQUES, AREA OF IMPROVEMENTS, ETC.)

_____

_____

_____

SWIM LOG

DATE: _____ TIME: _____

BEGINNER ◯ INTERMEDIATE ◯ ADVANCED ◯

WARM UP	REPS	DISTANCE	TIME

SWIMMING STYLE	REPS	DISTANCE	TIME

COOL DOWN	REPS	DISTANCE	TIME

TOTAL:

NOTES: (TECHNIQUES, AREA OF IMPROVEMENTS, ETC.)

_____

_____

SWIM LOG

DATE: _____   TIME: _____

BEGINNER ◯   INTERMEDIATE ◯   ADVANCED ◯

WARM UP	REPS	DISTANCE	TIME

SWIMMING STYLE	REPS	DISTANCE	TIME

COOL DOWN	REPS	DISTANCE	TIME
TOTAL:			

NOTES: (TECHNIQUES, AREA OF IMPROVEMENTS, ETC.)

_____

_____

SWIM LOG

DATE: _____ TIME: _____

BEGINNER ◯ INTERMEDIATE ◯ ADVANCED ◯

WARM UP	REPS	DISTANCE	TIME

SWIMMING STYLE	REPS	DISTANCE	TIME

COOL DOWN	REPS	DISTANCE	TIME
TOTAL:			

NOTES: (TECHNIQUES, AREA OF IMPROVEMENTS, ETC.)

_____

_____

_____

SWIM LOG

DATE: _____   TIME: _____

BEGINNER ◯   INTERMEDIATE ◯   ADVANCED ◯

WARM UP	REPS	DISTANCE	TIME

SWIMMING STYLE	REPS	DISTANCE	TIME

COOL DOWN	REPS	DISTANCE	TIME
TOTAL:			

NOTES: (TECHNIQUES, AREA OF IMPROVEMENTS, ETC.)

_____

_____

_____

SWIM LOG

DATE: _____ TIME: _____

BEGINNER ◯ INTERMEDIATE ◯ ADVANCED ◯

WARM UP	REPS	DISTANCE	TIME

SWIMMING STYLE	REPS	DISTANCE	TIME

COOL DOWN	REPS	DISTANCE	TIME

TOTAL: _____

NOTES: (TECHNIQUES, AREA OF IMPROVEMENTS, ETC.)

_____

_____

_____

SWIM LOG

DATE: _____ TIME: _____

BEGINNER ◯ INTERMEDIATE ◯ ADVANCED ◯

WARM UP	REPS	DISTANCE	TIME

SWIMMING STYLE	REPS	DISTANCE	TIME

COOL DOWN	REPS	DISTANCE	TIME
TOTAL:			

NOTES: (TECHNIQUES, AREA OF IMPROVEMENTS, ETC.)

_____

_____

_____

SWIM LOG

DATE: _____   TIME: _____

BEGINNER ⭕   INTERMEDIATE ⭕   ADVANCED ⭕

WARM UP	REPS	DISTANCE	TIME

SWIMMING STYLE	REPS	DISTANCE	TIME

COOL DOWN	REPS	DISTANCE	TIME
TOTAL:			

NOTES: (TECHNIQUES, AREA OF IMPROVEMENTS, ETC.)

_____

_____

SWIM LOG

DATE: _____ TIME: _____

BEGINNER ◯ INTERMEDIATE ◯ ADVANCED ◯

WARM UP	REPS	DISTANCE	TIME

SWIMMING STYLE	REPS	DISTANCE	TIME

COOL DOWN	REPS	DISTANCE	TIME
TOTAL:			

NOTES: (TECHNIQUES, AREA OF IMPROVEMENTS, ETC.)

_____

_____

_____

SWIM LOG

DATE: .... TIME: ....

BEGINNER ◯   INTERMEDIATE ◯   ADVANCED ◯

WARM UP	REPS	DISTANCE	TIME

SWIMMING STYLE	REPS	DISTANCE	TIME

COOL DOWN	REPS	DISTANCE	TIME
TOTAL:			

NOTES: (TECHNIQUES, AREA OF IMPROVEMENTS, ETC.)

SWIM LOG

DATE: _____   TIME: _____

BEGINNER ◯   INTERMEDIATE ◯   ADVANCED ◯

WARM UP	REPS	DISTANCE	TIME

SWIMMING STYLE	REPS	DISTANCE	TIME

COOL DOWN	REPS	DISTANCE	TIME
TOTAL:			

NOTES: (TECHNIQUES, AREA OF IMPROVEMENTS, ETC.)

_____

_____

SWIM LOG

DATE: _____   TIME: _____

BEGINNER ◯   INTERMEDIATE ◯   ADVANCED ◯

WARM UP	REPS	DISTANCE	TIME

SWIMMING STYLE	REPS	DISTANCE	TIME

COOL DOWN	REPS	DISTANCE	TIME

TOTAL: _____

NOTES: (TECHNIQUES, AREA OF IMPROVEMENTS, ETC.)

_____

_____

_____

SWIM LOG

DATE: _____   TIME: _____

BEGINNER ⭕   INTERMEDIATE ⭕   ADVANCED ⭕

WARM UP	REPS	DISTANCE	TIME

SWIMMING STYLE	REPS	DISTANCE	TIME

COOL DOWN	REPS	DISTANCE	TIME
TOTAL:			

NOTES: (TECHNIQUES, AREA OF IMPROVEMENTS, ETC.)

_____

_____

SWIM LOG

DATE: _____   TIME: _____

BEGINNER ◯   INTERMEDIATE ◯   ADVANCED ◯

WARM UP	REPS	DISTANCE	TIME

SWIMMING STYLE	REPS	DISTANCE	TIME

COOL DOWN	REPS	DISTANCE	TIME
TOTAL:			

NOTES: (TECHNIQUES, AREA OF IMPROVEMENTS, ETC.)

_____

_____

SWIM LOG

DATE: .... TIME: ....

BEGINNER ◯   INTERMEDIATE ◯   ADVANCED ◯

WARM UP	REPS	DISTANCE	TIME

SWIMMING STYLE	REPS	DISTANCE	TIME

COOL DOWN	REPS	DISTANCE	TIME
TOTAL:			

NOTES: (TECHNIQUES, AREA OF IMPROVEMENTS, ETC.)

....

....

....

SWIM LOG

DATE: .... TIME: ....

BEGINNER ◯ INTERMEDIATE ◯ ADVANCED ◯

WARM UP	REPS	DISTANCE	TIME

SWIMMING STYLE	REPS	DISTANCE	TIME

COOL DOWN	REPS	DISTANCE	TIME
TOTAL:			

NOTES: (TECHNIQUES, AREA OF IMPROVEMENTS, ETC.)

....

....

....

SWIM LOG

DATE: _____ TIME: _____

BEGINNER ◯ INTERMEDIATE ◯ ADVANCED ◯

WARM UP	REPS	DISTANCE	TIME

SWIMMING STYLE	REPS	DISTANCE	TIME

COOL DOWN	REPS	DISTANCE	TIME

TOTAL:

NOTES: (TECHNIQUES, AREA OF IMPROVEMENTS, ETC.)

_____

_____

_____

SWIM LOG

DATE: _____ TIME: _____

BEGINNER ◯   INTERMEDIATE ◯   ADVANCED ◯

WARM UP	REPS	DISTANCE	TIME

SWIMMING STYLE	REPS	DISTANCE	TIME

COOL DOWN	REPS	DISTANCE	TIME
TOTAL:			

NOTES: (TECHNIQUES, AREA OF IMPROVEMENTS, ETC.)

_____

_____

SWIM LOG

DATE: _____   TIME: _____

BEGINNER ◯   INTERMEDIATE ◯   ADVANCED ◯

WARM UP	REPS	DISTANCE	TIME

SWIMMING STYLE	REPS	DISTANCE	TIME

COOL DOWN	REPS	DISTANCE	TIME
TOTAL:			

NOTES: (TECHNIQUES, AREA OF IMPROVEMENTS, ETC.)

_____

_____

_____

SWIM LOG

DATE: _____ TIME: _____

BEGINNER ◯ INTERMEDIATE ◯ ADVANCED ◯

WARM UP	REPS	DISTANCE	TIME

SWIMMING STYLE	REPS	DISTANCE	TIME

COOL DOWN	REPS	DISTANCE	TIME
TOTAL:			

NOTES: (TECHNIQUES, AREA OF IMPROVEMENTS, ETC.)

_____

_____

SWIM LOG

DATE: _____ TIME: _____

BEGINNER ◯   INTERMEDIATE ◯   ADVANCED ◯

WARM UP	REPS	DISTANCE	TIME

SWIMMING STYLE	REPS	DISTANCE	TIME

COOL DOWN	REPS	DISTANCE	TIME
TOTAL:			

NOTES: (TECHNIQUES, AREA OF IMPROVEMENTS, ETC.)

_____

_____

_____

SWIM LOG

DATE: _____   TIME: _____

BEGINNER ◯   INTERMEDIATE ◯   ADVANCED ◯

WARM UP	REPS	DISTANCE	TIME

SWIMMING STYLE	REPS	DISTANCE	TIME

COOL DOWN	REPS	DISTANCE	TIME
TOTAL:			

NOTES: (TECHNIQUES, AREA OF IMPROVEMENTS, ETC.)

_____

_____

SWIM LOG

DATE: _____   TIME: _____

BEGINNER ⭕   INTERMEDIATE ⭕   ADVANCED ⭕

WARM UP	REPS	DISTANCE	TIME

SWIMMING STYLE	REPS	DISTANCE	TIME

COOL DOWN	REPS	DISTANCE	TIME
TOTAL:			

NOTES: (TECHNIQUES, AREA OF IMPROVEMENTS, ETC.)

_____

_____

_____

SWIM LOG

DATE: _____   TIME: _____

BEGINNER ◯   INTERMEDIATE ◯   ADVANCED ◯

WARM UP	REPS	DISTANCE	TIME

SWIMMING STYLE	REPS	DISTANCE	TIME

COOL DOWN	REPS	DISTANCE	TIME

TOTAL:

NOTES: (TECHNIQUES, AREA OF IMPROVEMENTS, ETC.)

_____

_____

SWIM LOG

DATE: _____   TIME: _____

BEGINNER ◯   INTERMEDIATE ◯   ADVANCED ◯

WARM UP	REPS	DISTANCE	TIME

SWIMMING STYLE	REPS	DISTANCE	TIME

COOL DOWN	REPS	DISTANCE	TIME
TOTAL:			

NOTES: (TECHNIQUES, AREA OF IMPROVEMENTS, ETC.)

_____

_____

_____

SWIM LOG

DATE: _____ TIME: _____

BEGINNER ◯ INTERMEDIATE ◯ ADVANCED ◯

WARM UP	REPS	DISTANCE	TIME

SWIMMING STYLE	REPS	DISTANCE	TIME

COOL DOWN	REPS	DISTANCE	TIME

TOTAL:

NOTES: (TECHNIQUES, AREA OF IMPROVEMENTS, ETC.)

SWIM LOG

DATE: _____   TIME: _____

BEGINNER ⬤   INTERMEDIATE ⬤   ADVANCED ⬤

WARM UP	REPS	DISTANCE	TIME

SWIMMING STYLE	REPS	DISTANCE	TIME

COOL DOWN	REPS	DISTANCE	TIME

TOTAL: _____

NOTES: (TECHNIQUES, AREA OF IMPROVEMENTS, ETC.)

SWIM LOG

DATE: _____   TIME: _____

BEGINNER ◯   INTERMEDIATE ◯   ADVANCED ◯

WARM UP	REPS	DISTANCE	TIME

SWIMMING STYLE	REPS	DISTANCE	TIME

COOL DOWN	REPS	DISTANCE	TIME
TOTAL:			

NOTES: (TECHNIQUES, AREA OF IMPROVEMENTS, ETC.)

_____

_____

SWIM LOG

DATE: _____   TIME: _____

BEGINNER ⃝   INTERMEDIATE ⃝   ADVANCED ⃝

WARM UP	REPS	DISTANCE	TIME

SWIMMING STYLE	REPS	DISTANCE	TIME

COOL DOWN	REPS	DISTANCE	TIME
TOTAL:			

NOTES: (TECHNIQUES, AREA OF IMPROVEMENTS, ETC.)

_____

_____

_____

SWIM LOG

DATE: _____ TIME: _____

BEGINNER ◯ INTERMEDIATE ◯ ADVANCED ◯

WARM UP	REPS	DISTANCE	TIME

SWIMMING STYLE	REPS	DISTANCE	TIME

COOL DOWN	REPS	DISTANCE	TIME
TOTAL:			

NOTES: (TECHNIQUES, AREA OF IMPROVEMENTS, ETC.)

_____

_____

_____

SWIM LOG

DATE: _____   TIME: _____

BEGINNER ◯   INTERMEDIATE ◯   ADVANCED ◯

WARM UP	REPS	DISTANCE	TIME

SWIMMING STYLE	REPS	DISTANCE	TIME

COOL DOWN	REPS	DISTANCE	TIME

TOTAL: _____

NOTES: (TECHNIQUES, AREA OF IMPROVEMENTS, ETC.)

_____

_____

SWIM LOG

DATE: _____   TIME: _____

BEGINNER ◯   INTERMEDIATE ◯   ADVANCED ◯

WARM UP	REPS	DISTANCE	TIME

SWIMMING STYLE	REPS	DISTANCE	TIME

COOL DOWN	REPS	DISTANCE	TIME
TOTAL:			

NOTES: (TECHNIQUES, AREA OF IMPROVEMENTS, ETC.)

_____

_____

SWIM LOG

DATE: _____ TIME: _____

BEGINNER ◯ INTERMEDIATE ◯ ADVANCED ◯

WARM UP	REPS	DISTANCE	TIME

SWIMMING STYLE	REPS	DISTANCE	TIME

COOL DOWN	REPS	DISTANCE	TIME
TOTAL:			

NOTES: (TECHNIQUES, AREA OF IMPROVEMENTS, ETC.)

_____

_____

SWIM LOG

DATE: _____   TIME: _____

BEGINNER ○   INTERMEDIATE ○   ADVANCED ○

WARM UP	REPS	DISTANCE	TIME

SWIMMING STYLE	REPS	DISTANCE	TIME

COOL DOWN	REPS	DISTANCE	TIME
TOTAL:			

NOTES: (TECHNIQUES, AREA OF IMPROVEMENTS, ETC.)

_____

_____

SWIM LOG

DATE: _____   TIME: _____

BEGINNER ◯   INTERMEDIATE ◯   ADVANCED ◯

WARM UP	REPS	DISTANCE	TIME

SWIMMING STYLE	REPS	DISTANCE	TIME

COOL DOWN	REPS	DISTANCE	TIME
TOTAL:			

NOTES: (TECHNIQUES, AREA OF IMPROVEMENTS, ETC.)

_____

_____

_____

SWIM LOG

DATE: _____ TIME: _____

BEGINNER ◯ INTERMEDIATE ◯ ADVANCED ◯

WARM UP	REPS	DISTANCE	TIME

SWIMMING STYLE	REPS	DISTANCE	TIME

COOL DOWN	REPS	DISTANCE	TIME

TOTAL:

NOTES: (TECHNIQUES, AREA OF IMPROVEMENTS, ETC.)

_____

_____

SWIM LOG

DATE: _____   TIME: _____

BEGINNER ◯   INTERMEDIATE ◯   ADVANCED ◯

WARM UP	REPS	DISTANCE	TIME

SWIMMING STYLE	REPS	DISTANCE	TIME

COOL DOWN	REPS	DISTANCE	TIME

TOTAL: _____

NOTES: (TECHNIQUES, AREA OF IMPROVEMENTS, ETC.)

_____

_____

_____

SWIM LOG

DATE: _____ TIME: _____

BEGINNER ◯   INTERMEDIATE ◯   ADVANCED ◯

WARM UP	REPS	DISTANCE	TIME

SWIMMING STYLE	REPS	DISTANCE	TIME

COOL DOWN	REPS	DISTANCE	TIME
TOTAL:			

NOTES: (TECHNIQUES, AREA OF IMPROVEMENTS, ETC.)

_____

_____

SWIM LOG

DATE: _____   TIME: _____

BEGINNER ◯   INTERMEDIATE ◯   ADVANCED ◯

WARM UP	REPS	DISTANCE	TIME

SWIMMING STYLE	REPS	DISTANCE	TIME

COOL DOWN	REPS	DISTANCE	TIME
TOTAL:			

NOTES: (TECHNIQUES, AREA OF IMPROVEMENTS, ETC.)

_____

_____

_____

SWIM LOG

DATE: _____ TIME: _____

BEGINNER ⭘ INTERMEDIATE ⭘ ADVANCED ⭘

WARM UP	REPS	DISTANCE	TIME

SWIMMING STYLE	REPS	DISTANCE	TIME

COOL DOWN	REPS	DISTANCE	TIME
TOTAL:			

NOTES: (TECHNIQUES, AREA OF IMPROVEMENTS, ETC.)

_____

_____

SWIM LOG

DATE: _____   TIME: _____

BEGINNER ◯   INTERMEDIATE ◯   ADVANCED ◯

WARM UP	REPS	DISTANCE	TIME

SWIMMING STYLE	REPS	DISTANCE	TIME

COOL DOWN	REPS	DISTANCE	TIME
TOTAL:			

NOTES: (TECHNIQUES, AREA OF IMPROVEMENTS, ETC.)

_____

_____

_____

SWIM LOG

DATE: _____ TIME: _____

BEGINNER ◯   INTERMEDIATE ◯   ADVANCED ◯

WARM UP	REPS	DISTANCE	TIME

SWIMMING STYLE	REPS	DISTANCE	TIME

COOL DOWN	REPS	DISTANCE	TIME
TOTAL:			

NOTES: (TECHNIQUES, AREA OF IMPROVEMENTS, ETC.)

_____

_____

SWIM LOG

DATE: _____   TIME: _____

BEGINNER ◯   INTERMEDIATE ◯   ADVANCED ◯

WARM UP	REPS	DISTANCE	TIME

SWIMMING STYLE	REPS	DISTANCE	TIME

COOL DOWN	REPS	DISTANCE	TIME

TOTAL: _____

NOTES: (TECHNIQUES, AREA OF IMPROVEMENTS, ETC.)

_____

_____

_____

SWIM LOG

DATE: _____   TIME: _____

BEGINNER ◯   INTERMEDIATE ◯   ADVANCED ◯

WARM UP	REPS	DISTANCE	TIME

SWIMMING STYLE	REPS	DISTANCE	TIME

COOL DOWN	REPS	DISTANCE	TIME
TOTAL:			

NOTES: (TECHNIQUES, AREA OF IMPROVEMENTS, ETC.)

_____

_____

_____

SWIM LOG

DATE: _____ TIME: _____

BEGINNER ◯   INTERMEDIATE ◯   ADVANCED ◯

WARM UP	REPS	DISTANCE	TIME

SWIMMING STYLE	REPS	DISTANCE	TIME

COOL DOWN	REPS	DISTANCE	TIME
TOTAL:			

NOTES: (TECHNIQUES, AREA OF IMPROVEMENTS, ETC.)

_____

_____

_____

SWIM LOG

DATE: _____   TIME: _____

BEGINNER ⭘   INTERMEDIATE ⭘   ADVANCED ⭘

WARM UP	REPS	DISTANCE	TIME

SWIMMING STYLE	REPS	DISTANCE	TIME

COOL DOWN	REPS	DISTANCE	TIME
TOTAL:			

NOTES: (TECHNIQUES, AREA OF IMPROVEMENTS, ETC.)

_____

_____

_____

SWIM LOG

DATE: _____ TIME: _____

BEGINNER ◯ INTERMEDIATE ◯ ADVANCED ◯

WARM UP	REPS	DISTANCE	TIME

SWIMMING STYLE	REPS	DISTANCE	TIME

COOL DOWN	REPS	DISTANCE	TIME
TOTAL:			

NOTES: (TECHNIQUES, AREA OF IMPROVEMENTS, ETC.)

_____

_____

_____

SWIM LOG

DATE: _____   TIME: _____

BEGINNER ◯   INTERMEDIATE ◯   ADVANCED ◯

WARM UP	REPS	DISTANCE	TIME

SWIMMING STYLE	REPS	DISTANCE	TIME

COOL DOWN	REPS	DISTANCE	TIME

TOTAL:

NOTES: (TECHNIQUES, AREA OF IMPROVEMENTS, ETC.)

_____

_____

_____

SWIM LOG

DATE: .... TIME: ....

BEGINNER ◯ INTERMEDIATE ◯ ADVANCED ◯

WARM UP	REPS	DISTANCE	TIME

SWIMMING STYLE	REPS	DISTANCE	TIME

COOL DOWN	REPS	DISTANCE	TIME

TOTAL:

NOTES: (TECHNIQUES, AREA OF IMPROVEMENTS, ETC.)

SWIM LOG

DATE: _____   TIME: _____

BEGINNER ◯   INTERMEDIATE ◯   ADVANCED ◯

WARM UP	REPS	DISTANCE	TIME

SWIMMING STYLE	REPS	DISTANCE	TIME

COOL DOWN	REPS	DISTANCE	TIME
TOTAL:			

NOTES: (TECHNIQUES, AREA OF IMPROVEMENTS, ETC.)

_____

_____

_____

SWIM LOG

DATE: _____   TIME: _____

BEGINNER ◯   INTERMEDIATE ◯   ADVANCED ◯

WARM UP	REPS	DISTANCE	TIME

SWIMMING STYLE	REPS	DISTANCE	TIME

COOL DOWN	REPS	DISTANCE	TIME
TOTAL:			

NOTES: (TECHNIQUES, AREA OF IMPROVEMENTS, ETC.)

_____

_____

_____

SWIM LOG

DATE: _____   TIME: _____

BEGINNER ◯   INTERMEDIATE ◯   ADVANCED ◯

WARM UP	REPS	DISTANCE	TIME

SWIMMING STYLE	REPS	DISTANCE	TIME

COOL DOWN	REPS	DISTANCE	TIME
TOTAL:			

NOTES: (TECHNIQUES, AREA OF IMPROVEMENTS, ETC.)

_____

_____

SWIM LOG

DATE: _____   TIME: _____

BEGINNER ◯   INTERMEDIATE ◯   ADVANCED ◯

WARM UP	REPS	DISTANCE	TIME

SWIMMING STYLE	REPS	DISTANCE	TIME

COOL DOWN	REPS	DISTANCE	TIME

TOTAL: _____

NOTES: (TECHNIQUES, AREA OF IMPROVEMENTS, ETC.)

_____

_____

_____

SWIM LOG

DATE: _____ TIME: _____

BEGINNER ⬭ INTERMEDIATE ⬭ ADVANCED ⬭

WARM UP	REPS	DISTANCE	TIME

SWIMMING STYLE	REPS	DISTANCE	TIME

COOL DOWN	REPS	DISTANCE	TIME
TOTAL:			

NOTES: (TECHNIQUES, AREA OF IMPROVEMENTS, ETC.)

_____

_____

SWIM LOG

DATE: _____ TIME: _____

BEGINNER ◯ INTERMEDIATE ◯ ADVANCED ◯

WARM UP	REPS	DISTANCE	TIME

SWIMMING STYLE	REPS	DISTANCE	TIME

COOL DOWN	REPS	DISTANCE	TIME
TOTAL:			

NOTES: (TECHNIQUES, AREA OF IMPROVEMENTS, ETC.)

_____

_____

_____

SWIM LOG

DATE: _____ TIME: _____

BEGINNER ◯   INTERMEDIATE ◯   ADVANCED ◯

WARM UP	REPS	DISTANCE	TIME

SWIMMING STYLE	REPS	DISTANCE	TIME

COOL DOWN	REPS	DISTANCE	TIME
TOTAL:			

NOTES: (TECHNIQUES, AREA OF IMPROVEMENTS, ETC.)

_____

_____

_____

SWIM LOG

DATE: _____ TIME: _____

BEGINNER ◯ INTERMEDIATE ◯ ADVANCED ◯

WARM UP	REPS	DISTANCE	TIME

SWIMMING STYLE	REPS	DISTANCE	TIME

COOL DOWN	REPS	DISTANCE	TIME
TOTAL:			

NOTES: (TECHNIQUES, AREA OF IMPROVEMENTS, ETC.)

_____

_____

_____

SWIM LOG

DATE: _____   TIME: _____

BEGINNER ○   INTERMEDIATE ○   ADVANCED ○

WARM UP	REPS	DISTANCE	TIME

SWIMMING STYLE	REPS	DISTANCE	TIME

COOL DOWN	REPS	DISTANCE	TIME
TOTAL:			

NOTES: (TECHNIQUES, AREA OF IMPROVEMENTS, ETC.)

_____

_____

_____

SWIM LOG

DATE: _____ TIME: _____

BEGINNER ◯ INTERMEDIATE ◯ ADVANCED ◯

WARM UP	REPS	DISTANCE	TIME

SWIMMING STYLE	REPS	DISTANCE	TIME

COOL DOWN	REPS	DISTANCE	TIME
TOTAL:			

NOTES: (TECHNIQUES, AREA OF IMPROVEMENTS, ETC.)

_____

_____

SWIM LOG

DATE: _____ TIME: _____

BEGINNER ◯ INTERMEDIATE ◯ ADVANCED ◯

WARM UP	REPS	DISTANCE	TIME

SWIMMING STYLE	REPS	DISTANCE	TIME

COOL DOWN	REPS	DISTANCE	TIME
TOTAL:			

NOTES: (TECHNIQUES, AREA OF IMPROVEMENTS, ETC.)

_____

_____

SWIM LOG

DATE: _____   TIME: _____

BEGINNER ◯   INTERMEDIATE ◯   ADVANCED ◯

WARM UP	REPS	DISTANCE	TIME

SWIMMING STYLE	REPS	DISTANCE	TIME

COOL DOWN	REPS	DISTANCE	TIME
TOTAL:			

NOTES: (TECHNIQUES, AREA OF IMPROVEMENTS, ETC.)

SWIM LOG

DATE: _____ TIME: _____

BEGINNER ◯ INTERMEDIATE ◯ ADVANCED ◯

WARM UP	REPS	DISTANCE	TIME

SWIMMING STYLE	REPS	DISTANCE	TIME

COOL DOWN	REPS	DISTANCE	TIME
TOTAL:			

NOTES: (TECHNIQUES, AREA OF IMPROVEMENTS, ETC.)

_____

_____

_____

SWIM LOG

DATE: _____   TIME: _____

BEGINNER ◯   INTERMEDIATE ◯   ADVANCED ◯

WARM UP	REPS	DISTANCE	TIME

SWIMMING STYLE	REPS	DISTANCE	TIME

COOL DOWN	REPS	DISTANCE	TIME

TOTAL: _____

NOTES: (TECHNIQUES, AREA OF IMPROVEMENTS, ETC.)

_____

_____

_____

SWIM LOG

DATE: _____   TIME: _____

BEGINNER ◯   INTERMEDIATE ◯   ADVANCED ◯

WARM UP	REPS	DISTANCE	TIME

SWIMMING STYLE	REPS	DISTANCE	TIME

COOL DOWN	REPS	DISTANCE	TIME
TOTAL:			

NOTES: (TECHNIQUES, AREA OF IMPROVEMENTS, ETC.)

_____

_____

_____

SWIM LOG

DATE: _____ TIME: _____

BEGINNER ◯ INTERMEDIATE ◯ ADVANCED ◯

WARM UP	REPS	DISTANCE	TIME

SWIMMING STYLE	REPS	DISTANCE	TIME

COOL DOWN	REPS	DISTANCE	TIME

TOTAL: _____

NOTES: (TECHNIQUES, AREA OF IMPROVEMENTS, ETC.)

_____

_____

_____

SWIM LOG

DATE: _____   TIME: _____

BEGINNER ◯   INTERMEDIATE ◯   ADVANCED ◯

WARM UP	REPS	DISTANCE	TIME

SWIMMING STYLE	REPS	DISTANCE	TIME

COOL DOWN	REPS	DISTANCE	TIME
TOTAL:			

NOTES: (TECHNIQUES, AREA OF IMPROVEMENTS, ETC.)

_____

_____

_____

SWIM LOG

DATE: _____ TIME: _____

BEGINNER ◯   INTERMEDIATE ◯   ADVANCED ◯

WARM UP	REPS	DISTANCE	TIME

SWIMMING STYLE	REPS	DISTANCE	TIME

COOL DOWN	REPS	DISTANCE	TIME

TOTAL: _____

NOTES: (TECHNIQUES, AREA OF IMPROVEMENTS, ETC.)

_____

_____

_____

SWIM LOG

DATE: _____   TIME: _____

BEGINNER ◯   INTERMEDIATE ◯   ADVANCED ◯

WARM UP	REPS	DISTANCE	TIME

SWIMMING STYLE	REPS	DISTANCE	TIME

COOL DOWN	REPS	DISTANCE	TIME
TOTAL:			

NOTES: (TECHNIQUES, AREA OF IMPROVEMENTS, ETC.)

_____

_____

SWIM LOG

DATE: _____ TIME: _____

BEGINNER ◯　　INTERMEDIATE ◯　　ADVANCED ◯

WARM UP	REPS	DISTANCE	TIME

SWIMMING STYLE	REPS	DISTANCE	TIME

COOL DOWN	REPS	DISTANCE	TIME
TOTAL:			

NOTES: (TECHNIQUES, AREA OF IMPROVEMENTS, ETC.)

_____

_____

SWIM LOG

DATE: _____   TIME: _____

BEGINNER ◯   INTERMEDIATE ◯   ADVANCED ◯

WARM UP	REPS	DISTANCE	TIME

SWIMMING STYLE	REPS	DISTANCE	TIME

COOL DOWN	REPS	DISTANCE	TIME
TOTAL:			

NOTES: (TECHNIQUES, AREA OF IMPROVEMENTS, ETC.)

_____

_____

_____

SWIM LOG

DATE: .... TIME: ....

BEGINNER ◯ INTERMEDIATE ◯ ADVANCED ◯

WARM UP	REPS	DISTANCE	TIME

SWIMMING STYLE	REPS	DISTANCE	TIME

COOL DOWN	REPS	DISTANCE	TIME
TOTAL:			

NOTES: (TECHNIQUES, AREA OF IMPROVEMENTS, ETC.)

....

....

....

SWIM LOG

DATE: _____   TIME: _____

BEGINNER ⃝   INTERMEDIATE ⃝   ADVANCED ⃝

WARM UP	REPS	DISTANCE	TIME

SWIMMING STYLE	REPS	DISTANCE	TIME

COOL DOWN	REPS	DISTANCE	TIME
TOTAL:			

NOTES: (TECHNIQUES, AREA OF IMPROVEMENTS, ETC.)

_____

_____

_____

SWIM LOG

DATE: _____   TIME: _____

BEGINNER ⬭   INTERMEDIATE ⬭   ADVANCED ⬭

WARM UP	REPS	DISTANCE	TIME

SWIMMING STYLE	REPS	DISTANCE	TIME

COOL DOWN	REPS	DISTANCE	TIME
TOTAL:			

NOTES: (TECHNIQUES, AREA OF IMPROVEMENTS, ETC.)

_____

_____

_____

SWIM LOG

DATE: .... TIME: ....

BEGINNER ◯   INTERMEDIATE ◯   ADVANCED ◯

WARM UP	REPS	DISTANCE	TIME

SWIMMING STYLE	REPS	DISTANCE	TIME

COOL DOWN	REPS	DISTANCE	TIME
TOTAL:			

NOTES: (TECHNIQUES, AREA OF IMPROVEMENTS, ETC.)

....

....

....

SWIM LOG

DATE: .... TIME: ....

BEGINNER ◯ INTERMEDIATE ◯ ADVANCED ◯

WARM UP	REPS	DISTANCE	TIME

SWIMMING STYLE	REPS	DISTANCE	TIME

COOL DOWN	REPS	DISTANCE	TIME
TOTAL:			

NOTES: (TECHNIQUES, AREA OF IMPROVEMENTS, ETC.)

....

....

....

SWIM LOG

DATE: _____ TIME: _____

BEGINNER ◯   INTERMEDIATE ◯   ADVANCED ◯

WARM UP	REPS	DISTANCE	TIME

SWIMMING STYLE	REPS	DISTANCE	TIME

COOL DOWN	REPS	DISTANCE	TIME

TOTAL:

NOTES: (TECHNIQUES, AREA OF IMPROVEMENTS, ETC.)

SWIM LOG

DATE: _____   TIME: _____

BEGINNER ◯   INTERMEDIATE ◯   ADVANCED ◯

WARM UP	REPS	DISTANCE	TIME

SWIMMING STYLE	REPS	DISTANCE	TIME

COOL DOWN	REPS	DISTANCE	TIME
TOTAL:			

NOTES: (TECHNIQUES, AREA OF IMPROVEMENTS, ETC.)

_____

_____

SWIM LOG

DATE: _____   TIME: _____

BEGINNER ⃝   INTERMEDIATE ⃝   ADVANCED ⃝

WARM UP	REPS	DISTANCE	TIME

SWIMMING STYLE	REPS	DISTANCE	TIME

COOL DOWN	REPS	DISTANCE	TIME

TOTAL: _____

NOTES: (TECHNIQUES, AREA OF IMPROVEMENTS, ETC.)

_____

_____

_____

SWIM LOG

DATE: .... TIME: ....

BEGINNER ◯ INTERMEDIATE ◯ ADVANCED ◯

WARM UP	REPS	DISTANCE	TIME

SWIMMING STYLE	REPS	DISTANCE	TIME

COOL DOWN	REPS	DISTANCE	TIME
TOTAL:			

NOTES: (TECHNIQUES, AREA OF IMPROVEMENTS, ETC.)

....

....

SWIM LOG

DATE: _____   TIME: _____

BEGINNER ◯   INTERMEDIATE ◯   ADVANCED ◯

WARM UP	REPS	DISTANCE	TIME

SWIMMING STYLE	REPS	DISTANCE	TIME

COOL DOWN	REPS	DISTANCE	TIME
TOTAL:			

NOTES: (TECHNIQUES, AREA OF IMPROVEMENTS, ETC.)

_____

_____

_____

SWIM LOG

DATE: _____   TIME: _____

BEGINNER ◯   INTERMEDIATE ◯   ADVANCED ◯

WARM UP	REPS	DISTANCE	TIME

SWIMMING STYLE	REPS	DISTANCE	TIME

COOL DOWN	REPS	DISTANCE	TIME
TOTAL:			

NOTES: (TECHNIQUES, AREA OF IMPROVEMENTS, ETC.)

_____

_____

_____

SWIM LOG

DATE: _____ TIME: _____

BEGINNER ⬭ INTERMEDIATE ⬭ ADVANCED ⬭

WARM UP	REPS	DISTANCE	TIME

SWIMMING STYLE	REPS	DISTANCE	TIME

COOL DOWN	REPS	DISTANCE	TIME
TOTAL:			

NOTES: (TECHNIQUES, AREA OF IMPROVEMENTS, ETC.)

_____

_____

_____

SWIM LOG

DATE: _____   TIME: _____

BEGINNER ◯   INTERMEDIATE ◯   ADVANCED ◯

WARM UP	REPS	DISTANCE	TIME

SWIMMING STYLE	REPS	DISTANCE	TIME

COOL DOWN	REPS	DISTANCE	TIME
TOTAL:			

NOTES: (TECHNIQUES, AREA OF IMPROVEMENTS, ETC.)

_____

_____

_____

SWIM LOG

DATE: _____   TIME: _____

BEGINNER ◯   INTERMEDIATE ◯   ADVANCED ◯

WARM UP	REPS	DISTANCE	TIME

SWIMMING STYLE	REPS	DISTANCE	TIME

COOL DOWN	REPS	DISTANCE	TIME
TOTAL:			

NOTES: (TECHNIQUES, AREA OF IMPROVEMENTS, ETC.)

_____

_____

_____

SWIM LOG

DATE: _____   TIME: _____

BEGINNER ◯   INTERMEDIATE ◯   ADVANCED ◯

WARM UP	REPS	DISTANCE	TIME

SWIMMING STYLE	REPS	DISTANCE	TIME

COOL DOWN	REPS	DISTANCE	TIME

TOTAL: _____

NOTES: (TECHNIQUES, AREA OF IMPROVEMENTS, ETC.)

_____

_____

_____

SWIM LOG

DATE: _____ TIME: _____

BEGINNER ◯   INTERMEDIATE ◯   ADVANCED ◯

WARM UP	REPS	DISTANCE	TIME

SWIMMING STYLE	REPS	DISTANCE	TIME

COOL DOWN	REPS	DISTANCE	TIME
TOTAL:			

NOTES: (TECHNIQUES, AREA OF IMPROVEMENTS, ETC.)

_____

_____

_____

SWIM LOG

DATE: _____ TIME: _____

BEGINNER ◯   INTERMEDIATE ◯   ADVANCED ◯

WARM UP	REPS	DISTANCE	TIME

SWIMMING STYLE	REPS	DISTANCE	TIME

COOL DOWN	REPS	DISTANCE	TIME
TOTAL:			

NOTES: (TECHNIQUES, AREA OF IMPROVEMENTS, ETC.)

_____

_____

_____

SWIM LOG

DATE: _____ TIME: _____

BEGINNER ◯   INTERMEDIATE ◯   ADVANCED ◯

WARM UP	REPS	DISTANCE	TIME

SWIMMING STYLE	REPS	DISTANCE	TIME

COOL DOWN	REPS	DISTANCE	TIME

TOTAL:

NOTES: (TECHNIQUES, AREA OF IMPROVEMENTS, ETC.)

SWIM LOG

DATE: _____   TIME: _____

BEGINNER ◯   INTERMEDIATE ◯   ADVANCED ◯

WARM UP	REPS	DISTANCE	TIME

SWIMMING STYLE	REPS	DISTANCE	TIME

COOL DOWN	REPS	DISTANCE	TIME
TOTAL:			

NOTES: (TECHNIQUES, AREA OF IMPROVEMENTS, ETC.)

_____

_____

_____

SWIM LOG

DATE: _____ TIME: _____

BEGINNER ◯ INTERMEDIATE ◯ ADVANCED ◯

WARM UP	REPS	DISTANCE	TIME

SWIMMING STYLE	REPS	DISTANCE	TIME

COOL DOWN	REPS	DISTANCE	TIME
TOTAL:			

NOTES: (TECHNIQUES, AREA OF IMPROVEMENTS, ETC.)

_____

_____

_____

Made in the USA
Middletown, DE
17 December 2022